MW01227712

Religions throug...

Hinduism

Robert Jackson

Series editor: Clive Erricker

Longman

About the *Religions through Festivals* series

Festivals are ways of remembering who we are and where we belong. Religious festivals are ways in which people of one faith celebrate their belonging together.

These are not only times of great joy but also of serious reflection – two aspects of festivals which, when brought together, provide a clear way for people to understand the meaning of a faith for a believer and for a community.

This series looks at six great religious traditions – Hinduism, Buddhism, Islam, Christianity, Judaism and Sikhism – through their festivals. One thing that will become clear, when you read these books, is just how different each of the faiths is. With this in mind, each author has approached his or her task in the way best suited to convey a feeling for the specialness of each religion.

All six books are concerned, not only with conveying information, but also with ways of learning, because real understanding results from the way we learn as well as what we learn.

Each spread in each book offers plenty of variety for learning to take place, in the use of pictures and activities as well as text so that the skill of learning about a religious faith will grow progressively as you use and enjoy the books.

About *Hinduism*

This book is about a very old religion from India. Hinduism includes a great variety of different beliefs and practices and one way of describing it is as a loosely-knit tradition. It stretches over a vast country of over a million square miles with a great range of languages and cultures. When you think that Hinduism has also spread to other countries like Britain, the picture becomes even more complicated! This book gives something of the flavour of this religion through its festivals, which help to show its great variety. This is done by looking not only at celebrations in different parts of India but also at the life of a Gujarati Hindu family living in Britain and members of some other British Hindu families too.

Front cover: *A woman drinks water that has been offered to the gods, during the Arti ceremony.*

Contents

1 An alien looks on

● Get into a group of between three and five friends and sit facing one another. Have pen and paper ready. You have to imagine that you are aliens from another planet. You are very clever, you have X-ray vision and you are friendly. But you don't know anything about planet Earth, the beings that live on it, or the languages they speak. Your mission is to look for signs of life near your ship and to report back to your base commander with a short message describing what you think is happening. Your craft silently lands near the dwelling place of some earthlings. Using your X-ray vision you look through the walls. The scene you see is the one in the picture. Now, together with your friends, write a short message to your base commander describing what you think is happening. Spend about five minutes preparing the message. Don't read any further until you have written your message.

If other groups in your class have done the same task, take it in turns to read out the messages from the different groups.

Some questions

As you listen to these messages, in your group, do the following tasks:

– Make a list of the observations that the alien got wrong.

– Make a list of the observations that the alien got right.

– Can you think of some things that the alien would need to do in order to understand what is in the picture? Make a list of them.

In this book you are going to look at some festivals celebrated by Hindus in Britain and in India. You may not have looked at someone else's way of life before. Look again at your lists. What things do you need to do so you don't make the mistakes that the alien made when he observed the earthlings?

Hindu children observe Christmas

Hari (a boy) and Lila (a girl) are Hindu children who live in a fishing village in north India. They are working for the de Silvas, a Christian family from Bombay who have a bungalow in the village. The de Silvas have put a branch from a casuarina tree in a pot of sand.

Hari was puzzled to see it decked with bits of coloured paper that fluttered in the wind, and silver stars and gold balls that spun and bobbed and danced. The group on the veranda was especially gay and excited and loud that evening as grown-ups played games with children and they all sang and laughed till late at night. They ate their dinner very late and Hari reported how, while washing dishes in the kitchen, he had seen them set fire to a ball of food on a plate before eating it – he couldn't say why.

When Lila next went in to sweep, she had to clear away heaps of torn, coloured paper lying on the floor. As she carefully folded up the torn sheets and put them away in a neat heap, the mother came up and said, "Oh, just throw them away – Christmas is over." Puzzled, Lila carried away the paper to their hut for Bela and Kamal to see and use. "Christmas is over," she said and, to her surprise, the girls knew what that meant and nodded. "Yes, Christmas. Our teacher told us about it at school. It is the birthday feast of a baby who was born long, long ago in a stable," said Bela. "Like Krishna who was born in a prison," explained Kamal when Lila looked puzzled. "But why did they cover the tree with coloured paper and stars?" she asked, and they could not answer: their teacher had said nothing about a tree.

from The Village by the Sea *by Anita Desai, Puffin*

● Write down three things you think Hari and Lila could do in order to understand Christmas better.

2   **Photo puzzle**

● Look carefully at the picture. Unless all the things you can see in the picture are familiar to you, imagine that you have to work out what is happening using intelligent guess work – like the alien who looked at the Christmas tree.

Some questions

– In which country was the picture taken?
– In what sort of building are the people sitting?
– What types of musical instruments can you see (e.g. strings, keyboard, percussion)? Can you guess the names of any of the instruments?
– Guess what kind of books they are.
– What do you think the people are doing?
– Why do you think there are only men?

Inside a Hindu temple

The picture was taken in England. (Did you notice the suits and sweaters which might have given you a clue?) The people are sitting in a Hindu temple. It used to be a school, so a school or community centre would have been good guesses.

You can see two percussion instruments – some little cymbals (called **manjira**) and a pair of drums (called **tabla**). There is a keyboard instrument called a **harmonium**. This is a portable organ into which air is pumped with one hand, while the keyboard is played with the other. You might have guessed that the tall, stringed instrument is a sitar. What you can see is really a **tambura**, which looks rather like a sitar but is simpler and easier to play.

The books (not the booklets) are copies of one Hindu sacred book. There are lots of different sacred books in Hinduism, though only a few are used widely. This one is a story about a prince called **Rama** and a princess called **Sita**. The book is called the "**Ramayana**" (pronounced with the stress on the second, not the third "a").

The people are singing part of the "Ramayana". It is written as a long poem. They are meeting to sing a section every day for a month until the book is finished.

There are only men because the picture shows only part of the room. The women are sitting on the other side. As they face the front, the men are on the right and the women on the left. This is the custom in many Hindu temples and in other Asian places of worship, including some Christian churches.

Hindus in Britain

Hinduism is the religion of about 80 per cent of the 800 million people who live in India, and it can claim to be the oldest religion in the world. At various times, Hindus have gone to live and work in other countries. There are more than 350 000 Hindus in the United Kingdom. Some came here from states of India such as **Gujarat** and the **Punjab**. Others migrated to African countries such as Uganda and Kenya and later moved to Britain. On the next page we meet Mrs Lodhia whose parents moved from Gujarat in India to Uganda. She later moved to England and got married. You will also meet her children, Sejal and Deepesh. Like many other young Hindus, they are British born and bred.

Key Words

manjira tabla harmonium
tambura Rama Sita
"Ramayana" Gujarat Punjab

3 Divali

Divali (it rhymes with barley) is the most widely-celebrated festival in India and usually occurs in October or November. The word Divali means "row of lights" and stories connected with light are told at the festival. Perhaps the most common is about **Lakshmi**, the goddess of wealth. It is said that if you light up your house with lamps (**divas**), Lakshmi will visit you and bring you prosperity and good fortune, if you behave properly. Hindus perform an act of worship or **puja** to Lakshmi at Divali. The pictures show Madhu Lodhia performing Lakshmi puja at her home in Coventry. On the left, she is anointing coins with yoghurt which Hindus regard as a very pure substance. The pot of water, coloured powders and **betel leaf** are all offered to Lakshmi. On the right, Madhu is placing a **chandlo** (a red mark) on Lakshmi's forehead to show her devotion to the goddess.

Remembering Divali

Madhu Lodhia was brought up in Uganda. In 1965, Madhu came to live in England. Here she remembers Divali during her childhood in Uganda.

"We'd wake up at five o'clock in the morning on Divali day and clean the house – everybody was so busy and happy. There were lots of sweets and savouries and we'd send some on a **thali** (a metal tray) round to other houses, and people would send gifts of sweets back. We used to get new dresses and jewellery and we used to send Divali cards to relations in Kenya or in India.

"We used to go out in the evening. The shops were open till 12 o'clock at night and the streets were decorated with banana plants and different coloured electric lights. In the shops Lakshmi puja was going on. People wore nice clothes and they would let off fireworks. We'd go to a shop to buy some colourful bangles or some dress material. We used to have four days' holiday from school at Divali time. Girls used to decorate outside the shops on the ground or outside the house with coloured chalks or powders. They'd draw water lilies or an attractive pattern – the word for this is **rangoli**. The best would get a prize.

"We left the windows open so Lakshmi could get in and we would put lights (divas) in the windows to attract her."

Divali in England

Here are comments by two Hindu children in England.

Chetan (boy)	"It's when you get all your presents, and when you give presents as well, and that's why I like it. It's nice wrapping them up and giving them to the person."
Chetna (girl)	"Divali, that's my favourite. We have fireworks and we have lamps on the walls, and we sometimes have a party and bring relatives and make special food."

Key Words

Lakshmi diva puja
betel leaf chandlo
thali rangoli

● On page 5 there is a story about Hari and Lila finding out about Christmas. Using the information you have just read about Divali, write a story about Hari and Lila celebrating Divali for children who have never heard of Divali before.

4 Festivals through the year

Look carefully at the picture. The object consists of lots of pages, held together with a big metal staple. No pages are missing.

- What do you think the object is?
- You have been told that no pages are missing. Does this surprise you in any way?
- In what language do you think the non-English words and numbers are written?

Hindu calendars

The object is a calendar – the sort with a page for each day of the year. The day shown is 5 November 1983, which was Guy Fawkes night or bonfire night in Britain. The page we can see shows the first day of the year. The official calendar used in Britain is the Gregorian calendar, which has New Year on 1 January. The calendar in the picture is an Indian calendar which divides the year up differently from the Gregorian calendar. The Indian year varies slightly in length from year to year, so New Year is not on the same Gregorian date each year. It happened to be New Year's Day on 5 November 1983 for the Hindus who use this calendar.

Hindus in various regions of India use different calendars. This one is used by people who live (or whose families used to live) in Gujarat state. The non-English words on the calendar are written in the Gujarati language – one of the 14 main languages of India. With most Indian calendars, New Year occurs in March or April, but on the Gujarati calendar it comes in October or November just after the Divali festival. This is why Divali is sometimes known as a New Year festival.

- Find out more about the Gregorian calendar and how it works.

- Find out more about the Indian calendars and how they work.

Time

One reason why science fiction stories such as "Dr Who" are popular is that they take a different view of time from the one we usually have. Dr Who can travel backwards and forwards in time. Sometimes religions take unusual views of time which make us take a fresh look at the ways in which we live. In Hindu mythology one human year is one day to the gods. The gods' year is 360 of ours. Twelve thousand years of the gods make up one group of four ages. At the end of the fourth age, the world is destroyed and the cycle starts all over again . . . and again . . . and again. This myth, or story, can help Hindus to see that their hopes and worries, though important, are only a tiny drop in the ocean of life.

- With a group of friends make a list of any stories, books, TV programmes or films you know that deal with the subject of time. Choose a sub-title for each one which tells something about how the story or programme deals with time. For example: "Dr Who – Backwards and Forwards in Time".

- As festivals are repeated each year, they keep alive stories, customs and teachings. Find out the date of the next important Hindu festival that will happen this year. Plan a reconstruction of the festival. This could be presented to the school in an assembly.

5 Rama and Sita

Rama defeats the demon king Ravana

The story of Rama

The story of Rama is connected with several festivals. In some parts of India it is one of the stories told at Divali. The children in the pictures above are from an infant school in Coventry. They have been acting the story in the open air.

Many years ago, in India, there lived a king called Dasratha who ruled over the kingdom of Ayodhya. He had three wives and four sons. The eldest son, Rama, was heir to the throne. Rama was really the god Vishnu in human form. His task was to rid the world of demons, especially the ten-headed demon king Ravana.

Queen Kaikeyi, Dasratha's favourite wife, was jealous because

Rama was to become king. She told lies about Rama, so that Dasratha would make her son the king. Dasratha believed her and he banished Rama from the kingdom for 14 years. Kaikeyi's son was angry with his mother because of the lies she told about Rama. He took Rama's golden sandals and put them on the throne to show that it was really Rama's and said, "I will look after Rama's kingdom until he returns and removes the sandals from the throne."

Rama had a beautiful wife named Sita. Because of the dangers he would have to face, Rama decided to leave Sita with his mother. Sita loved Rama dearly and insisted that she should be by his side. Finally, Rama agreed to take Sita with him along with his brother, **Lakshmana**. Off they went to live in the forest.

One day, while Rama and Lakshmana were out hunting, the demon king **Ravana** changed himself into a holy man. In this disguise he tricked Sita into coming close to him. Ravana seized her, changed back to his true self and carried Sita away to the island of Lanka.

When the brothers found out what had happened they swore they would find Sita and kill Ravana. **Hanuman**, the monkey king, promised to help Rama and he sent out his monkeys to look for Sita. A small monkey soon returned with the news that Sita and Ravana were on the island of Lanka.

The brothers and the monkeys set off for Lanka. When they came to the sea Hanuman used his special powers to leap across it. He was followed by the others, who built a bridge with their own bodies. The brothers crossed over the bridge to the island. After 10 days of fierce fighting, Rama finally killed Ravana.

Sita was overjoyed to see Rama. They returned to Ayodhya immediately, now that the 14 years of exile were over. The people lit divas throughout the city to welcome Rama and Sita home. Rama's brother took the golden sandals from the throne so that Rama could sit in his rightful place, with Sita beside him.

Things to do

Key Words
Lakshmana
Ravana   Hanuman

- Draw a comic-strip version of the story, using only pictures. Think carefully about which incidents you think are important. Now cut out your pictures so that they are all separate. Shuffle them. Then ask your partner to put them in the right order and re-tell the story to you.

- Write down one thing about Sita and one thing about Rama that you think Hindus would admire.

- Make up your own version of the story. You may be able to record it on a cassette recorder. Play the tape to a younger child, perhaps a brother or sister.

6 Festival food

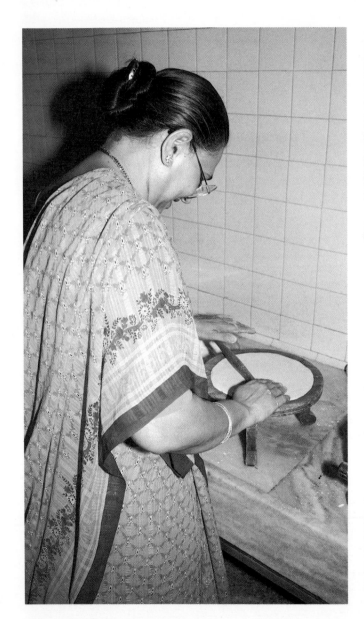 

Above left *Mrs Soni, Mrs Lodhia's sister, making chapatis at her home in Bombay.*
Above right *Tejal, her daughter, cooks chapatis on a tawa.*

Festivals are often times when families have the chance to meet together for a celebration meal. Indian meals include many different dishes – rice dishes, sweets, a variety of breads and savoury dishes seasoned with spices. Indian cooks do not use curry powder (which is a mixture of spices) but prefer to mix their own spices. Indian dishes do not have to be hot. Chilli is the only really hot spice.

14

Chapatis

Chapatis are a kind of unleavened bread (i.e. no yeast is added). They are cooked on a **tawa**, an iron griddle, but a thick-bottomed frying pan will do instead. Special flour for making chapatis can be bought from Asian grocery stores, but wholemeal flour or a half and half mixture of wholemeal and plain flour is a good substitute. This is a recipe that will make eight chapatis. One pound (450g) of flour will make about 30 chapatis.

115 g (4 oz) flour – for the dough
up to 115 ml (4 fl oz) water
about 60 g (2 oz) flour for dusting the chapatis

Place the flour in a bowl. Slowly add water and mix with hands until a stiff dough is formed. Do not make the dough too wet. Knead for 8 minutes, roll into a ball and cover the bowl with a damp tea towel or with cling film. Leave for at least half an hour. Put the tawa or frying pan on to medium heat. While it is heating, divide the dough into eight balls and cover them with a damp cloth. Flour a rolling board, dip one of the balls in the dry flour and roll into a round chapati – about 15 cm in diameter. Indian cooks produce circular chapatis – beginners will have to do their best! Place the uncooked chapati on the tawa or frying pan. As soon as it bubbles (about 30 seconds), use tongs to turn the chapati over and leave for another 30 seconds. The chapatis can be served immediately or stacked (either plain or lightly buttered) and wrapped in foil where they will keep warm for about 20 minutes.

Spicy potatoes

450 g (1 lb) potatoes, peeled and cut into bite size pieces
1 medium sized onion, peeled and chopped finely
1 clove garlic, chopped finely
3 tablespoons vegetable oil (e.g. ground nut)
1 level teaspoon each of turmeric; ground coriander seed and
    ground cumin seed
½ teaspoon salt
1 tablespoon of chopped coriander leaves *or* chopped parsley
3 tablespoons plain yoghurt
1 teacup (200 ml) water

Heat the oil and gently fry the onion and garlic for 4 minutes. Add the spices and continue to fry gently for 1 minute. Add the potatoes and fry for 1 minute. Add a teacup of cold water and the salt and stir in the yoghurt. Bring to the boil and simmer until the potatoes are tender. Sprinkle chopped coriander leaves or parsley on the dish before serving. Serve with chapatis.

Key Words
chapati   tawa

7 The Lodhia family

In the picture Mr and Mrs Lodhia and their two children Sejal, a 14-year-old girl, and Deepesh, a 12-year-old boy, are having a meal at the time of a festival. Two generations ago, all the Lodhia family lived in what is now Gujarat state in India. But some members of the family migrated to other countries. Mrs Lodhia was born in Uganda; Mr Lodhia was brought up in Aden.

Hindu families

In Britain, people are used to thinking of parents and their children as a family. Among Hindu communities the family normally includes more people and is often called the **joint family**. Usually there would be an older man and his wife. Then there would be the couple's sons, with their wives and children. There might also be one or more unmarried daughters.

Family ties are close, and you are expected to be responsible for all the members of your family. In many parts of India, your first cousins are called your cousin-brothers or cousin-sisters. They are treated much more like western people would treat brothers and sisters than they would cousins.

In English there are no special words to show whether an aunt is your father's sister or mother's sister, or whether a grandfather is your mother's father or father's father. In the Indian languages there are special words to show the relationship between all the different members of the family. Imagine an 11-year-old girl called Seema, who speaks the Hindi language. Seema's mother's sister would be **Mausiji**, but the aunt who is married to her father's elder brother would be **Taiji**. The ending "ji" is added to each word to show respect and affection.

Mr and Mrs Lodhia's family are scattered in several countries, but they keep in close touch with each other, and visit one another when they can. Sejal's cousin-sister, Tejal, has travelled from Bombay to stay with her in Coventry, and Sejal and Deepesh have been to India to visit members of the family.

The Lodhia family's mother-tongue is **Gujarati**, one of the 14 main languages of India. The Lodhias, like Seema, also speak **Hindi** and are fluent in English.

All the Lodhias belong to the same **caste**, a grouping of many families. Some castes have ancestors who did the same kind of job. The Lodhias' ancestors were goldsmiths. Some members of the family are still in the jewellery business. Usually Hindus marry someone from the same caste, and parents help to find suitable partners for their children.

● Pick out five important words in the passage about Hindu families and explain them to the person next to you.

Vegetarianism

Many Hindus do not eat meat. The Lodhias are vegetarians and none of the food you can see in the picture contains meat, fish or even eggs. The vast majority of Hindus do not eat beef since the cow is regarded as a sacred animal. It stands for gentleness and simplicity and it provides wholesome food (milk, butter and yoghurt).

Key Words

joint family   Mausiji
Taiji   Gujarati
Hindi   caste

● Using a cassette recorder, a group of you can make a radio programme about vegetarianism. Interview members of your class who have different views. Write a short introduction to the programme and link together the interviews.

8 Pongal

Sweet rice pudding is prepared to offer to Surya, the sun god, during the festival of Pongal.

Most Hindu festivals follow the lunar calendar. There are some, however, that follow the movement of the sun. Of these the most important is held when the sun enters the sign of Capricorn, a date around 12 January. In the South Indian state of Tamil Nadu this festival is called **Pongal**.

Celebrating Pongal

As well as being a time of festivity and fun, Pongal shows the people's thanks for things on which they depend for their food. On the day before Pongal, old or unwanted possessions are burnt on a bonfire. On the first day, rice boiled with milk and sugar is offered to **Surya**, the sun god, as a thanksgiving for the harvest. It is this activity that gives the festival its name because the word Pongal in the Tamil language means "it has boiled". New clothes are worn as befits a day of new beginnings. On the second day, cattle are washed, garlanded and their sides and horns are decorated with paint. Then they are taken in procession. They are not made to work, but are honoured with prayers. On the third day, people visit friends, or travel from villages to visit the towns and cities.

● Make a list of reasons why you think cows are honoured at Pongal.

Caring for living things

Many Hindus believe in **rebirth**. This means that when a person dies he or she is reborn as another living thing. To harm anything living – not just a person – is thought of as injuring another fellow being. Also many Hindu sacred books say that God is present in all living beings and that we should therefore respect all creatures, whether human or animal.

Things to do

● On your own or with a small group of friends:

– Make a list of reasons why many Hindus show respect for the natural world and for living things.

– Write down three reasons why you think that it is important to care for the environment and for living things.

Compare your lists with those done by friends or other groups.

– Read through your first list and see if you can put some of the ideas into a picture or poster.

Key Words   Pongal   Surya   rebirth

9 Festival sweets

The picture shows trays of sweets at Mr Mehta's shop in Coventry. Sweets and sweet dishes can be eaten as snacks or may form part of a meal. For thousands of years Hindus have often included sweets in the things they offer to the gods during puja or worship. After worship the sweets are given out and the worshippers share in the god's blessing. Festivals – like Divali and Raksha Bandhan – are favourite times for giving sweets.

Indian sweets are of many different kinds. Some are toffee-like, many are fudges of one sort or another, and others are covered in a delicious syrup. Different regions of India have their own specialities and their own favourite ways of making sweets. Mr Mehta's family came originally from Gujarat and the sweets made and sold in his shop are favourites there. Many of them are also well-known to people from other parts of India.

Make your own sweets

One popular Indian sweet is **barfi**, a kind of fudge. It comes in different types and flavours. The kind in our recipe is easy to make. Even so, you will need help from your teacher or a parent because boiling sugar syrup is very dangerous. The amounts given in the recipe are enough for your classmates to have a bite each. If you want to make a smaller amount of barfi, halve all the quantities in the recipe.

Coconut barfi

255 g (9 oz) sugar
115 g (4 oz) desiccated coconut
8 tablespoons water
60 g (2 oz) dried full cream milk powder
1 tablespoon chopped pistachio nuts
or flaked almonds (optional).
A few drops of green, red or yellow food colouring.

1 Using butter or vegetable margarine, grease a flat metal baking tin.
2 Bring the water to the boil in a non-stick pan. Add the sugar and stir with a wooden spoon until a syrup forms. Bring to the boil and simmer gently for three minutes.
3 Add the coconut, the milk powder and a few drops of food colouring to the syrup. Mix thoroughly and heat gently until the mixture is very thick. Pour into the greased baking tin. You will need to scrape the last of the barfi out of the pan. Scatter chopped nuts (optional) over the barfi and then allow it to cool. Cut the barfi into bite-size pieces.

Things to do

● Think of a reason why the recipe does not use margarine made with animal fat.

● Think of a reason why milk is thought by Hindus to be a good food. If you can't think of any reasons, read the passage on vegetarianism (page 17) and try again.

● In the picture look for a calendar showing a Hindu god with an elephant's head. Turn to page 36 to find out about him.

Key Word barfi

10 Mahashivratri

Shiva

Shiva is one of the most important gods in Hinduism. Shiva has the power to create and to destroy. Sometimes he is pictured dancing in a circle of flames. There is a story that says it is the energy of Shiva's dance that created the world, that keeps the world in existence and that will destroy the world. Then Shiva will start to dance again and the cycle of creation, preservation and destruction will happen over and over again. In some stories it is said that Shiva performed this dance on Mahashivratri, which means "Great Night of Shiva".

Water being poured over a Shiva linga at Mahashivratri, at the Ram Mandir (temple), Coventry.

Shiva is often represented by the **linga**, a pillar-shaped piece of stone which shows his creative side. You can see a linga in the picture, surrounded by the coils of a cobra. The hooded head of the cobra acts as a canopy over the linga. A man is offering water to Shiva. You can see him pouring it from a copper vessel.

You can also see a coconut resting on a bed of betel leaves on a copper water pot. The coconut represents all the gods and goddesses, and the water in the pot stands for India's holy rivers. The **betel nuts** arranged around the pot represent the nine planets. The coconut and water pot were used in a puja to Ganesha which took place before the worship of Shiva. Ganesha is a son of Shiva. You can read a story about his birth on page 37.

In some stories Shiva is pictured as a holy man, living a simple life and spending a lot of time meditating and doing **yoga**. He has a powerful third eye in the middle of his forehead and he carries a trident. Pictures show him with his hair piled high on his head and his body smeared with ashes. Hindu holy men who worship Shiva often wear their hair in the same way. Sometimes pictures show the river Ganges flowing out of Shiva's hair. A story tells that the goddess Ganga (that is, the river Ganges) flowed towards the earth and was in danger of destroying it. Shiva broke the river's fall with his hair and so saved the world. Pictures of Shiva sometimes show his wife Parvati by his side.

● Most Hindus use **images** or pictures of gods and goddesses when they worship. Write down some reasons why using images might help them to worship. Compare your answers with other people in your class.

● Many religious people do not use pictures or images when they worship, and some believe that it is wrong to use them. Write down reasons why they might believe it is wrong to use images in worship. Compare your answers with others.

Fasting

During some festivals (including Mahashivratri) and at other times as well, Hindus may **fast**. This does not mean going without food entirely, but avoiding certain foods and only eating a little. Fasting helps self-control. It is also a reminder to Hindus of their devotion to God. In devotion to Shiva some Hindus fast on Mondays; on Mahashivratri itself, the whole family may fast. You are not supposed to eat cooked meals but you can have peanuts, fruit and barfi – so fasting is not too difficult!

● Find out about fasting in Christianity and Islam. Find out what foods are avoided, when the fasts take place and why people fast.

Key Words

linga   betel nut
yoga   images
fast

11 Holi

Krishna playing Holi with the gopis.

Holi is a festival in which you are allowed to drench everyone with coloured water or cover them with brightly coloured powder! In Hindu stories, even the gods celebrate Holi. In the picture you can see Lord Krishna doing playful battle with the **gopis**, the cowherd girls he grew up with in the town of Vrindaban.

24

Mrs Lodhia
remembers Holi

"Holi is my favourite festival. We had a holiday from school on Holi day and the festival lasted one day in Uganda. We'd get together with our friends and mix coloured water, and then we'd throw it over each other! Sometimes we'd throw glasses of coloured water. Other times we'd use syringes. We'd wear old clothes and start playing at about two and go on till six. We even threw colours over the Headteacher! We used to use a plant that coloured the water orange. After playing Holi we'd shower, put on new clothes and go to the temple. There'd be a bonfire and we'd put coconuts, popcorn and channa (chick peas) on it. Later we'd eat some of the roasted coconut as **prasad** – that's food that's been offered to God. We'd carry small children and babies around the fire. But throwing paint was the best part. When I went to India two years ago I played Holi for the first time for 18 years, since I came to England. Even old people were playing. But it's too cold to do it here!"

British Hindu
children on Holi

Chetan   "We go to the temple and we pray and sing songs called **bhajans**. At home we throw colour on each other – mostly dry, but we can squirt it as well. We sometimes use washing-up liquid bottles as squirters. We squirt colour on everybody, so people don't wear their best clothes on that day. We go to the temple and throw coconuts on the bonfire. Then we take them off and eat them."

Sejal   "I went to India two years ago, and we played colours at Holi. We wore old clothes – I wore my cousin's nightie – and we threw water balloons and sprayed people. We got up early in the morning, and it went on all day."

- Holi is a festival that allows you to break some of the rules of behaviour you are expected to keep for the rest of the year. Find out from your parents or grandparents whether they can remember any customs in the area in which they grew up that allowed them to break some of the usual rules.*

- Design and paint a poster to show the fun and carefree spirit of Holi.

Key Words

gopis prasad
bhajan

* Iona and Peter Opie's The Lore and Language of School Children (OUP, 1959) has some good examples.

12   A Holi story

People standing around the bonfire at Holi in Coventry.

Nilesh (a boy) said this about Holi:

"My name is Nilesh, I am eleven and a half years old and I live in Coventry. At Holi we build a fire like at bonfire night. We go in the temple first and sing songs, then we go outside and light the fire. We throw coconuts and dry rice on the fire and when the coconuts are cooked, we take them off and eat them. My mum sometimes tells us a story about a boy called Prahlad."

The story of Prahlad

There was once a demon king called Hiranyakashipu, which means "dressed in gold". The King had a son, Prahlad, who refused to worship his father, but instead worshipped the great god Vishnu. Prahlad's devotion to Vishnu sent the King into a rage and he decided to have the boy killed because he would not change his ways. The King ordered an army to cut Prahlad to pieces with their razor sharp swords. As the soldiers advanced, Prahlad called "Vishnu, Vishnu" and the soldiers lost their strength and were unable to kill the boy. Next, the King had Prahlad thrown into a pit of loathsome, poisonous snakes. Again the boy called the name of Vishnu and the snakes did him no harm. The King tried many other ways to get rid of the boy, once by trying to drown him in the sea and another time by having him trampled to death by a herd of giant elephants who lived in the skies. Every time the boy survived by calling the name of Vishnu. In desperation, the King summoned his sister Holika to help get rid of the boy. Holika was a demoness who once had been given a special favour by Agni, the fire god, so that she would always be protected from the dangers of fire. Holika tricked Prahlad into climbing with her on to an unlit bonfire. When they had climbed up, Holika grabbed the boy and called the King's soldiers to light the fire. The evil demoness cackled with laughter as the flames began to rise. Prahlad called: "Vishnu, Vishnu". The power of Vishnu was so great that Prahlad was protected from the flames, while Holika, in spite of her wish, perished in the fire.

Things to talk about

Here are some things to talk about in a small group. Your ideas can be shared with the rest of the class and you can explain why you gave your answers. Remember, more than one answer may be right! Look at the picture and read the story before discussing them.

- Why do you think a bonfire is lit at the festival of Holi?
- Why do you think the story of Prahlad is told at Holi?
- Do you think the story really happened? Why might Hindus think the story is important?
- Can you think of a TV programme or film that reminds you of stories like this one?

Things to do

Choose an activity to do by yourself, in pairs or in small groups.

- Draw a comic-strip version of the story.
- Do a painting based on one of the incidents in the story.
- Write a simple version of the story you could tell to younger brothers, sisters or friends.

27

13   Puja

In the picture you can see Sejal Lodhia performing puja or worship at her home in Coventry. Many Hindus have a **shrine** in the home, so the members of the family can worship God on their own or together.

> *Sejal*   "After I've had a shower or bath, I light a lamp and some incense sticks. I put these on a tray in front of the pictures of the gods. The oil in the lamp is ghi – that's clarified butter – and the wick is made of cotton wool. The **incense** is very fragrant."

Sejal is making an offering of incense to the gods. You can see pictures of Krishna (with his flute), of the goddesses Lakshmi and **Saraswati** (playing a musical instrument) and Ambaji (carrying weapons and riding on a tiger).

As this puja is taking place at the time of a festival, there are some special offerings. There are sweets (barfi and halva) and a tray (thali) containing a picture of the word **Om**, written in the Sanskrit language. Om is a sacred sound used in prayer and meditation. Sejal's mother, Madhu, has made the shapes of the letters by using desiccated coconut dyed with different food colourings.

Preparing for puja

Before performing puja in the morning, Sejal has a shower. Hindus regard it as very important that they and all the things used in the puja are as pure and clean as possible. Sometimes Hindus have their home-shrine in the kitchen. This is an ideal place for a shrine because everything in the kitchen has to be pure, for the preparation of food.

Sejal's prayers include the Gayatri mantra. "Let us meditate on the splendour of the sun-god. May he give us insight." As Sejal says this prayer to herself in the Sanskrit language, she is carrying on a tradition of devotion that goes back thousands of years to the ancient worship of India. Sejal also silently says her own personal prayers, especially for the family.

The Lodhia family offer puja to several gods and goddesses, but look carefully at what Mrs Lodhia says:

> "There is only one God. There are different **reincarnations** and different names. And there are goddesses as well as gods. But there is only one God."

Things to do

● *Either* write in your own words what you think Mrs Lodhia means
or paint or draw a picture which you could use to explain to someone else what Mrs Lodhia means.

● With some friends, make a list of words that come into your head when you think of the word "worship". Try to re-arrange the list into groups of words that have something in common with each other. Your teacher can help you to compare your groups of words with those written by other people in the class.

Key Words

shrine incense
Saraswati
Om reincarnation

14 Raksha Bandhan

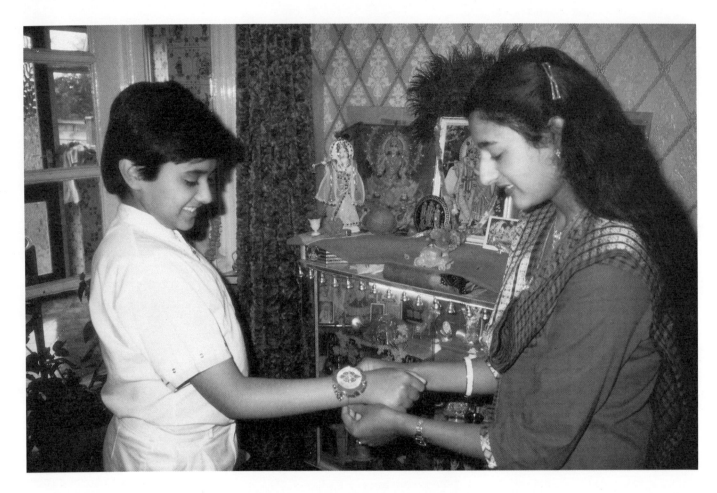

Raksha Bandhan is a festival for brothers and sisters. It takes place in July or August. "Raksha" means "protection" and "bandhan" means "to tie". In the picture you can see Sejal tying a **rakhi**, a kind of bracelet, on her brother Deepesh's right wrist. The rakhi stands for protection from harm.

Mrs Lodhia remembers

"Seeing the picture of my children reminds me of Raksha Bandhan when I was a child in Uganda. We'd get up early before my brother went to work. I'd tie a rakhi to my brother's wrist. In years gone by people used to make rakhis from red thread and white silk, but now we buy them. When we tied the rakhi we'd give a blessing. We were six sisters and five brothers and each sister would tie a rakhi on the wrist of every brother. One brother lived 15 miles away from our town of Jinja, in Kampala. I'd visit and tie a rakhi and he'd give me a gift – something made of gold, a sari or some money – usually things that you could remember him by. We'd make special food, such as chapatis stuffed with a sweet lentil mixture, mango juice, barfi and so on."

Children talk about Raksha Bandhan

Chetan (boy)	"Sisters tie a string with a flower on it or some kind of picture. They tie it on your right wrist. If you haven't got sisters, then your cousin-sisters do it. I've got a sister, but my cousin-sisters do it as well, so I get loads. They're mostly coloured red. Then the sisters give you some Indian sweets – they taste very nice. They say a silent prayer to God – they just do it in their minds – and say 'let my brother live for a long time'. My mum told me that they do this. We give the sisters a present, it might be a sari."
Keval (boy)	"I haven't got a sister so my cousin-sisters tie them. One year I had about ten. They give you sweets as well. If I want I can give them £5 or £1. My brother gives it for me."
Neema (girl)	"We send some rakhis off to Kenya, to my mum's two brothers and my cousin and they send me some money back."
Pankaj (boy)	"Your sister gives you a rakhi, a patterned thing, a bit like a watch, and ties it on your wrist and you have to give her some money. I don't really enjoy it, because I have to give her money!"

Things to do

- Look carefully at the picture. Using felt and red wool, design and make you own rakhi.

- Chetan and Keval mention cousin-sisters. Explain what this means. Look back at page 16 to remind yourself about cousin-brothers and cousin-sisters, if you cannot remember.

- If you are a girl, imagine that you are from a Hindu family in Britain. Write a letter to a cousin-brother in India at Raksha Bandhan. Pretend you are sending a rakhi with the letter.

- If you are a boy, imagine that you are from a Hindu family in Britain. Write a "thank you" letter to a cousin-sister in India who has sent you a rakhi. Pretend you are sending a gift with the letter.

Key Word

rakhi

15 Gods and goddesses

Marble images of Krishna and Radha

If you were asked to list the features which tell us what the word "bird" means, you might write something like this:
- has feathers   – most can fly
- warm blooded   – lays eggs

● Religious people talk about worshipping God. What do they mean by the word God? On your own, or with friends, make a list of the features that tell us what the word "God" means.

Do you have any of these points, or something like them?
- invisible   – superior to us
- you can't touch him   – created the Universe
- the most powerful being   – sometimes called "Father"
- the most loving being   – too hard to understand

This list might have been written by a Jew or a Christian. It shows God to be superior to humans, distant from them and impossible to understand completely. It also shows God as close to people and caring for them, as a good father cares for his children.

What do Hindus believe?

It is impossible to say what all Hindus believe about God, because not all Hindus share the same beliefs. Many Hindus would agree that we cannot fully understand God but that religious stories give us some idea of what God is like and how people should behave. These stories are mainly about gods (like Rama) and goddesses (like Lakshmi). Rama's honesty, loyalty and courage and Lakshmi's kindness show Hindus something about God and about how they should try and live. Hindus often feel that one particular god or goddess is special to them and helps them most to get close to God.

The god **Krishna** is special to very many Hindus, who believe that he came into the world to help people to live properly. Krishna is worshipped as a child (God loves people like a mother loves her child) and as the adviser to Prince Arjuna (in a book called ***Bhagavad Gita*** or *Song of God*). He is also worshipped as a young man, a flute-playing cowherd who loves the beautiful girl Radha. Their love gives worshippers some idea of the strength of God's love for them. If you look carefully at the picture you can see part of Krishna's flute. In the middle there is a smaller statue of Krishna.

Many Hindus believe that the gods Krishna and Rama are different forms of the great god Vishnu. You can read a story about Vishnu on page 27.

● Write a list of questions you think non-Hindus may need to ask in order to understand about Hindu gods and goddesses.

● In pairs, one of you explain to the other the picture opposite.

Key Words

Krishna
Bhagavad Gita

16 The languages of India

Not only has India lots of gods and lots of festivals, it also has lots of languages. India is a huge country of over a million square miles and about 800 million people. About four fifths of these are Hindus. India's regions are as varied as its languages. The festivals celebrated around India show this variety.

The country is divided into states, some of which have their own main language. In the southern state of Tamil Nadu, where the festival of Pongal is celebrated (see pages 18–19), the language is Tamil. In Maharashtra, where the celebration of Ganesha Chaturthi is popular, Marathi is spoken. Hindi is the official language in six of the northern states, although it is spoken in many dialects.

One language?

After Indian independence in 1947 the Government tried to make Hindi the national language. This never worked, mainly because the languages in the south (like Tamil) are very different from those in the north and people did not like having another language forced on them. However, Hindi is spoken widely as a second language, especially in northern states.

When the British controlled India as part of the British Empire, the English language became very important as a language that some people could speak and write no matter which part of India they came from. English is still used widely in India – in Parliament, for example.

Of the 350 000 plus Hindus who live in Britain, about 70 per cent can trace their ancestry back to the state of Gujarat in the north west. So Gujarati is a language spoken by a large minority of people in Britain today. Punjabi is spoken by about 15 per cent of Britain's Hindus, but also by Sikhs and (like Gujarati) by many Muslims. Hindi is spoken by many Hindus and Sikhs as a second language. Although it is written in a different way and has some words that are different, spoken Hindi and spoken Urdu (the official language of Pakistan) are very similar.

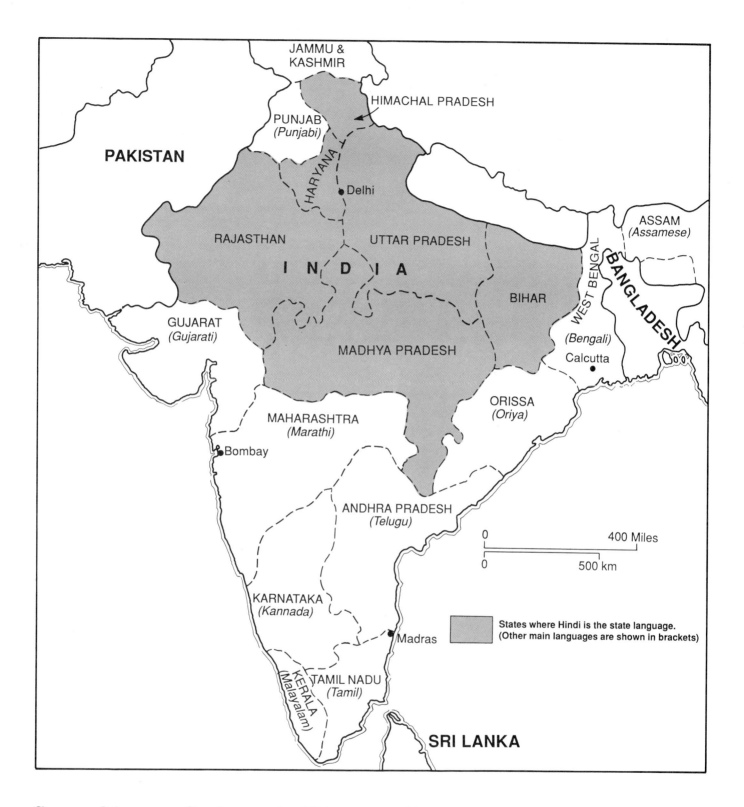

States where Hindi is the state language.
(Other main languages are shown in brackets)

Some things to find out

- With a group of friends, plan and carry out a survey of how many languages are spoken in your school.

- Some words from Indian languages have come into the English language. Find out the origin of these words: juggernaut mulligatawny bungalow.

17 Ganesha Chaturthi

Calendar picture of Ganesha

Ganesha Chaturthi celebrates the birth of Ganesha or Ganpati, a god with the head of an elephant and the body of a tubby man. The festival, which takes place in August or September, is especially popular in the state of Maharashtra (in west India).

Many Hindus pray to God in the form of Ganesha. Just as an elephant can use its great strength to remove obstacles in its path, Hindus believe Ganesha can help to overcome problems in their lives and protect them from harm. In pictures, Ganesha is often accompanied by a rat. The message here is that all beings have their place in life – whether big or small, strong or weak.

The elephant can trample everything in its path; the rat can squeeze through small holes to get the same results.

● Look carefully at the picture. Can you see the rat?
  – Why do you think Ganesha has four arms?
  – What is Ganesha holding in three of his hands and why do you think he is holding them?
  – Ganesha's fourth hand is held up with the palm towards you. What do you think this gesture means?

How Ganesha got his head

In Hindu stories, Ganesha is regarded as a son of the god Shiva. Here is one of several different stories that try to explain why Ganesha is like he is.

Shiva and Parvati had a son called Vinayaka. Every morning Parvati took a bath and while she was doing so guards stood by the door to make sure that no-one could enter. One day the guards were ill and Parvati asked her son to guard the door for her. She explained to him that on no account could anyone go in. Vinayaka stood proudly in front of the door with a large spear in his hand. He had not been on guard very long when he saw Shiva coming towards him. Vinayaka told him that Parvati had ordered that no-one was to enter. When Shiva realised he would not be allowed in, he developed the most terrible rage. He took his axe and chopped off his son's head.

Parvati, of course, was very upset about what had happened. When Shiva saw this he was sorry and looked around for Vinayaka's head so that he could try to put his son back together. The head was nowhere to be found. As Shiva was searching in the woods for the missing head, he met an elephant. Shiva asked the elephant if he would give his head so that the boy could live again. The elephant agreed.

Shiva returned to where his son's body lay and fixed the elephant's head on to it. Then he breathed life into it. The boy slowly sat up, rubbing his neck. Parvati was overjoyed to have her son given back to her. Lord Shiva announced from that day his son's new name would be Ganesha.

Information about Ganesha

The story explains Ganesha's strange appearance. The four arms show his power and enable him to carry various emblems: an axe (to remove obstacles) and a noose (used in India to catch wild elephants). Ganesha also holds one of his favourite sweets. His fourth hand is held in the gesture which means "Do not fear".

18 Janmashtami: Krishna's birthday

Janmashtami, at a Hindu temple in Coventry

Janmashtami is the festival which takes place in August or September celebrating the birth of Krishna. Many Hindus believe he is one of the forms of the god Vishnu. In the picture you can see a doll which represents the newborn Krishna in a swinging cradle. The time is midnight (the time of Krishna's birth) and worshippers have covered the image of Krishna with flowers as part of their worship of the divine child.

Deepesh writes about Janmashtami:

On 27 August it was Janmashtami and we celebrated it in our house. I got Lord Krishna's statue for my twelfth birthday and that day we took a half day off from school. My mum prepared some special food because everyone was fasting. There were about 30 ladies who came to my house to do **satsang** – meeting to pray and sing religious songs. My mum woke up about five o'clock and decorated the room where our shrine is. She decorated Krishna's statue with nice materials which she had sewn by hand and she even put imitation jewellery on him. Everyone sang hymns and played the tambourine. I took some photographs of the occasion. My aunt made a cradle out of a fruit basket, decorated with tinsel, balloons and coloured crêpe paper. The cradle was hanging from the ceiling with Krishna's statue inside it. It looked very colourful. I really enjoyed it that day.

● Pick out five words that you think would be especially important to Deepesh and explain them to a partner.

The birth of Krishna

There was once a cruel king called Kamsa. His sister Devaki married a nobleman called Vasudeva. A mysterious voice told Kamsa that he would be killed by a boy, the eighth child of Devaki and Vasudeva. Kamsa had Devaki and Vasudeva locked in prison for many years. During that time the couple had seven children and Kamsa had each of them put to death.

One dark and windy night, at midnight, an eighth child – a son – was born. A strange voice told Vasudeva to take the baby boy (whom they named Krishna) to the house of Nanda, chief of the cowherds, and his wife Yashoda and to bring back the baby girl he would find there. Miraculously, the guards did not wake up and the prison doors opened by themselves. Eventually, Vasudeva reached the village of Gokul where Nanda and Yashoda lived and he quietly exchanged the babies while everyone was asleep.

The next day Kamsa heard that a son had been born to Devaki and Vasudeva. Imagine the amazement when he discovered that the baby was a girl! Baby Krishna was brought up by Yashoda and Nanda. Despite many efforts by Kamsa to kill him, Krishna grew up to show people how they should love God and live a dutiful life.

Key Word

satsang

● Draw a comic-strip version of the story, using only pictures. Ask your partner to use the picture strip to retell the story.

19 Navratri

Mina   "Navratri means enjoying yourself, meeting friends,
(girl)   getting hot, staying up late and it's just fun."

Navratri ("nine nights") is one of the few festivals celebrated all over India. It is called by different names and celebrated in different ways (see pages 42–3 for Durga Puja). Most versions include the worship of the goddess and in some places the victory of Rama over Ravana is celebrated on the day after Navratri. This day is called **Dassehra**, which means "the tenth day".

Young women dancing dandia ras at Navratri at the Shree Krishna Temple in Coventry. The dancing goes on for nine nights in a row.

40

The stick dance

For Hindus who live (or whose families used to live) in Gujarat state, Navratri is a very important festival. It is a time for worshipping the goddess under one or more of her many names, or just called "**mataji**" which means "honoured mother". It is also a time for folk dancing and for fun.

Sejal (girl) "We dance in our best saris for the evening. The temple is usually crowded and looks very colourful. The thing I always look forward to is the stick dance. We have two circles of people who move in different directions and they hit sticks with the people opposite. These nine days are the most marvellous days in the year, because we meet new people. You get to know them better and you dance and sing."

Hansa "Ras is connected with Lord Krishna. Because he used to love doing ras with lots of gopis. Gopis are cowherd girls who Krishna knew when he was in Vrindaban. Lots of gopis used to dance with sticks and that's how it came about. As the evening goes on the ras gets faster and faster!

"**Garba** is another kind of dance. You clap your hands to the rhythm. Normally they praise the goddess and her beauty. Quite a few garbas you hear will have lots of goddesses' names mentioned."

Dandia ras and garba are danced around a special shrine to the goddess. It is a six-sided box with a cone-shaped top. On the top is a lamp inside a clay pot called a **garbo**. A picture of a different goddess is on each side of the box. The whole thing is decorated with coloured lights and tinsel. During the evening the **arti** ceremony is performed. Lots of brass lamps are circled in front of the shrine and other offerings are made, such as fruit and sweets. These are then given out as prasad, holy food which gives God's blessing to those who eat it.

Key Words

Dassehra   mataji
garba   dandia ras
garbo   arti

- Hinduism is one faith in which dance is used to praise God. Find out about the use of dance in worship in one or two other religions.

- Find out about the eating of food as part of worship in one or two other religions. Make a list of the similarities and differences with the arti ceremony.

20 Durga Puja

In the Indian state of West Bengal, Navratri is known as Durga Puja. The picture shows Bengalis who live in the Indian capital New Delhi taking an image of Durga to the festival. Images of Durga are worshipped for nine days. On the tenth day (Dassehra) they are taken to a river or pond and immersed in the water.

● Look carefully at the picture.
   – On what animal is Durga riding?
   – Why has Durga got lots of arms?

Durga and the buffalo demon

More than anything Mahisha, the buffalo demon, wanted to live for ever. So he went to Brahma, the creator god, and said "Lord, give me immortality". Brahma replied, "All who are born must die." Mahisha thought for a while. "Then, Lord, if I have to die, let it be at the hands of a woman." "Very well," Lord Brahma told him, "let it be so."

Mahisha was delighted for he could not imagine how any woman could kill him. "We will attack heaven itself," he told his men. "All the gods will bow before me." Mahisha and his demon army defeated the god Indra and his followers in a fierce battle. Mahisha sat on Indra's throne and proclaimed: "From now on I alone shall be worshipped."

Meanwhile, the gods assembled secretly at the home of Lord Shiva. "We are helpless against the evil Mahisha," they complained. "Why should evil triumph over goodness like this?" At that moment, an intense light began to shine from the gods' faces. The beams of light met in the middle of the room making a brilliant ball of brightness, out of which emerged a figure. It was a female form, with many arms. This was Durga. As Durga stood, Shiva offered her his own spear. Others gave her weapons with which to attack Mahisha until each of her countless hands held a fearsome instrument of death. Durga mounted the back of a lion and rode towards Mahisha's palace.

Mahisha strode out to meet her, sword in hand. "How dare you, a woman, threaten me?" he bellowed. "Tremble with fear, Mahisha," she replied. "I come armed by the gods. Remember what you said to Brahma – if I die let it be at the hands of a woman. Well, I am a woman. You will die at my hands."

Mahisha's men attacked Durga but as her lion strode through the warriors, she destroyed hundreds of them. Mahisha turned himself into the form of a fierce buffalo. He charged at Durga, snorting and bellowing as he ran. As he reached her, Durga leapt on him and pinned him down. Mahisha struggled to free himself and half of him, in his real form, began to emerge from the body of the buffalo. At this Durga struck and Mahisha fell dead at her feet. The gods filled the skies with their shouts of joyful victory. "Durga, we praise you!" they cried. "You are one who destroys evil and upholds goodness."

Children listening to the story of Durga and Mahisha.

- Explain to a visitor why Durga looks like she does and what she represents. Keep your explanation to five statements.

- Make up your own story that has the moral "Good finds a way to defeat evil in the end".

21 Visiting a temple

If you live near a town or city which has a Hindu temple or **mandir**, your teacher may be able to arrange a visit for you. It is good to visit a temple when lots of people are there, perhaps at a festival like Divali or Navratri. However, since these occasions are usually out of school time it is easier to visit during the day.

A pupil from a Warwickshire school interviewing the President of a Hindu temple in Coventry.

Hindu communities will make you very welcome, but you must take care to plan your visit properly.

The pupil in the picture and her classmates had written their questions out and practised with the tape recorder. After the visit, the children presented an assembly based on their experiences and they invited the President of the temple to be their guest. Part of the assembly was a mock television news report about the visit. This is what the children wrote:

On Friday 14 February we visited the Shree Krishna Temple in Coventry. There we interviewed the President, Mr Lad. The temple was a school room before it became a temple in 1966. Mr Lad came to England in 1968. Mr Lad usually eats Indian food every day, but he has tried English food and he said he likes vegetable soup, bread, chips and cake. Mr Lad is a happily married man and he has six children and nine grandchildren. He lives in a terraced house in Coventry. He was married in India. He says: "My marriage was like a king's procession!" Mr Lad goes to the temple first in the morning to wait for the priest, then in the evening for the evening arti, a service where they make offerings to the God. They decorate the temple like we decorate our houses at Christmas. The Hindus at this temple have five main festivals. Divali is Mr Lad's favourite. Although most Hindus are vegetarians Mr Lad eats some meat. But not meat from the cow because it is their sacred animal.

Planning your visit

Eleanor is being taught a stick dance by Amita at a temple during the Navratri festival.

mandir

- With a group of friends, make a list of things you should do when planning a visit to a Hindu temple. Then compare the list with the one here.

  – Learn as much as you can about Hinduism beforehand.
  – Give the temple committee plenty of notice.
  – Ask your teacher to discuss the purpose of your visit with the temple committee.
  – Wear smart clothes and remember that you have to take your shoes off before going into the room which contains the shrines.
  – The temple is a place of prayer and worship. Behave responsibly.
  – Ask permission if you want to take photographs or make tape recordings.
  – Practise the activities you want to do in the temple. These might include: photography; tape recording; notetaking; sketching.
  – After the visit write a thank you letter.

- If you are unable to visit a Hindu mandir, ask your teacher if he or she can get some slides or a video which show worship in a temple.

22 The Hindu year: calendar

Several different calendars are used in India. The system shown in the diagram has 12 lunar months, each divided into a "bright half" (from the new moon to the full moon) and a "dark half" (from the full moon to the next new moon). Each half month is 15 days long. The year on this system does not coincide exactly with the year according to the Gregorian calendar, so the date of a Hindu festival will vary from year to year.

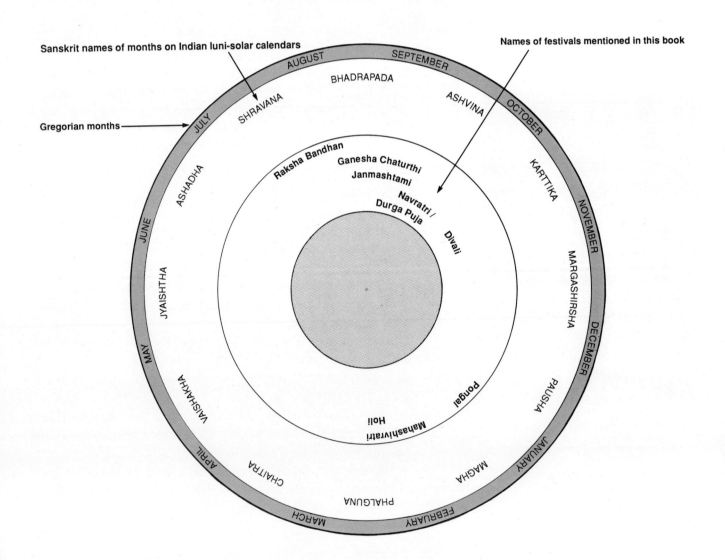

Sanskrit names of months on Indian luni-solar calendars

Names of festivals mentioned in this book

Gregorian months

AUGUST SEPTEMBER
BHADRAPADA
SHRAVANA ASHVINA OCTOBER
JULY
ASHADHA KARTTIKA
JUNE NOVEMBER
JYAISHTHA MARGASHIRSHA DECEMBER
MAY
VAISHAKHA PAUSHA
APRIL JANUARY
CHAITRA MAGHA
MARCH PHALGUNA FEBRUARY

Raksha Bandhan
Ganesha Chaturthi
Janmashtami
Navratri /
Durga Puja
Divali

Pongal
Mahashivratri
Holi

46

Glossary

Many Indian names come from the ancient language of Sanskrit. Speakers of modern Indian languages such as Hindi do not usually pronounce the last "a" in names such as Dasratha, Ganesha, Prahlada, Vasudeva. In fact, Rama and Shiva often rhyme with "calm" and "give" (not "calmer" and "giver"). In some names the final "a" is essential and must be heard clearly: examples are Sita, Radha, Yashoda.

Ambaji	Name of a goddess; the suffix "ji" shows affectionate respect.
arti	Worship in which a lamp (or lamps) is circled in front of pictures or statues of the gods.
barfi	Sweet which has sugar and milk as the main ingredients.
betel leaf	Large leaf which is used in worship.
betel nut	Nut, the size of a walnut, used in worship.
Bhagavad Gita	"Song of God" – one of the Hindu holy books.
caste	Large group of families – many castes have ancestors who shared the same occupation. Members of a caste may trace their ancestry back to the same important person. Normally, Hindus marry someone from the same caste.
chandlo	Gujarati word for a mark made on a worshipper's forehead and on pictures or *images* involved in an act of worship.
chapati	Flat, circular bread – cooked freshly for each meal and used to scoop up the food.
dandia ras	Stick dance popular among Gujarati Hindus.
Dassehra	"The tenth day", the day after Navratri.
diva (Hindi); divo (Gujarati)	Lamp, usually made of clay, fuelled with ghi (clarified butter) and having a cotton wool wick.
garba	Dance popular among Gujarati Hindus, especially at Navratri.
garbo	Clay pot containing a lamp that is placed on top of a portable shrine when Gujarati Hindus celebrate Navratri.
gopis	The cowherd girls who were friends of Krishna.
Hanuman	Monkey hero of the "Ramayana". Hanuman is also the god of strength.
harmonium	Keyboard instrument popular among Hindu communities.
images	Statues, pictures or other representations of a god or goddess.

incense	Substance which gives off a fragrant smell when burnt. It can be bought in packets of slender sticks.
joint family	Usually a pair of grandparents, their sons and daughters-in-law, and their grandchildren. There may also be one or more unmarried daughters.
Krishna	Name of a Hindu god who many believe to be an incarnation of the god Vishnu.
Lakshmi	Goddess of wealth and prosperity.
linga	Pillar-shaped stone used to represent the god Shiva.
mandir	Temple or small shrine in a Hindu's home.
mataji	"Honoured mother", a general name for the goddess.
Om	Sacred sound, uttered at the beginning of various prayers.
prasad	Food offered to and blessed by the gods which is then shared out among the worshippers.
puja	Worship in which offerings are made.
rakhi	Bracelet tied by a sister on her brother's wrist at Raksha Bandhan.
rangoli	Patterns made on the ground with coloured chalk or rice flour, usually at the festival of Divali.
Ravana	Ten-headed demon king who was defeated by Rama. (Remember to stress the first "a" in Ravana – it sounds like the "ar" in "park" – and not the second "a").
rebirth/ reincarnation	Being born again in another form, as a person or an animal.
tabla	Small drums, played as a pair using the fingers and palms of the hand.
tambura	Stringed instrument – the body is made from a gourd and the long neck from wood.
thali	Metal tray on which food is served or on which the articles used in *puja* are placed.
yoga	Physical and mental exercises used to improve the body and mind.